Original title:
Voyage Through the Inner

Author: Mirell Mesipuu
ISBN HARDBACK: 978-1-80560-956-8
ISBN PAPERBACK: 978-1-80561-517-0

A Journey Beneath the Stars

Beneath the blanket of the night,
Whispers of dreams take flight,
Wanderers dance among the glow,
In starlit tales, our hearts will flow.

Constellations guide the way,
As we roam where shadows play,
Moonlight drapes the world in peace,
In its embrace, our worries cease.

Galaxies spin in vibrant hues,
Telling stories of ancient views,
With every step, the vastness smiles,
Embracing hopes across the miles.

A comet's tail ignites the skies,
Leading us where wonder lies,
In the depth of cosmic seas,
We find our dreams, we find our keys.

Together, we chase the dawn,
In the silence, magic drawn,
For in the stars, we leave our mark,
A journey brightened by the spark.

Threads of Magic in the Inner Realm

In the hush of twilight's glow,
Whispers weave a tale we sow,
Colors dance in shadows' weave,
In this place, we dare believe.

Crimson threads of dreams align,
Stitching stories, yours and mine,
In secret chambers, spirits roam,
Guarding wishes we call home.

Glimmers shine where silence sways,
Magic pulses through the rays,
With every heartbeat, we are spun,
Threads of gold, united, one.

Winds of fate gently caress,
Unraveling fears, we confess,
Together we dive into the stream,
Where every shadow lights a dream.

Here within the inner maze,
Mysteries burst into a blaze,
We gather strength from the unknown,
Within this realm, we find our throne.

The Voyage Beyond the Horizon of Thought

Set sail toward the dawn's embrace,
Waves of wonder, time and space,
Horizons call with a siren's song,
To realms where thinkers all belong.

Chart the course through skies of gray,
Where ideas spark and shadows play,
With every wave, our minds expand,
In the ocean, wisdom stands.

Thoughts like currents pull us near,
To shores of dreams, free from fear,
We sail beneath the silver plume,
In the depths, our visions bloom.

Beyond the lines, we break away,
Embracing what the heart must say,
Together we'll chase the rising sun,
In this voyage, we are one.

With sails unfurled, we journey forth,
In pursuit of knowledge's worth,
The horizon whispers soft and sweet,
A promise where all seekers meet.

Journey of the Soul's Compass

In the heart of the misty dawn,
A compass guides where dreams are drawn.
Each step whispers tales untold,
Of treasures within, of courage bold.

Through valleys deep and mountains high,
The echoes of hope reach for the sky.
With every turn, the shadows flee,
As the spirit dances wild and free.

The journey leads through winding trails,
As the heart beats where love prevails.
In the silence, truths unfold,
In the warmth, the soul's gold.

Stars above the ocean's crest,
Point the way to quiet rest.
In the night, the fears will fade,
As the light of dawn unmade.

With each compass point anew,
The soul finds strength in the view.
From dawn to dusk, through night's embrace,
The journey weaves a sacred space.

The Uncharted Waters Within

Beneath the waves where silence sighs,
A world awaits, where courage lies.
In depths unseen, the heart must dive,
To find the will, to feel alive.

Currents pull with silent might,
Against the dark, I seek the light.
Each ripple speaks of dreams unchained,
In every storm, the soul regained.

Through shadows cast and fears that plead,
Learning to trust the heart's true need.
With every wave, a lesson learned,
In the quiet, my spirit burned.

The compass swings, the horizon calls,
In uncharted depths, the spirit thralls.
With each embrace of mysteries bold,
The river of life, a tale retold.

And in the end, I rise anew,
With stories rich and waters blue.
The uncharted realms, I now explore,
In my heart, a boundless shore.

Navigating the Depths of Self

In the stillness, whispers flow,
Mapping paths that gently glow.
Each thought, a star in night's expanse,
Guiding the heart in soulful dance.

Through labyrinths of doubt and grace,
I seek the truth, my rightful place.
In shadows deep, I find the key,
To unlock the depths inside of me.

The tides of time, they rise and fall,
Yet through the storm, I hear the call.
Each wave, a lesson, each swirl, a friend,
In the vastness, I start to mend.

Navigating fears, both bold and meek,
The voice within begins to speak.
In the mirror of the soul's vast sea,
I glimpse the world that's meant to be.

With every breath, I journey on,
Into the dusk, beyond the dawn.
The depths of self, an open door,
To find the treasure evermore.

Echoes from the Silent Abyss

In the silence where shadows play,
Echoes of silence gently sway.
Whispers linger, soft and low,
Reflecting all I've come to know.

From the depths of the darkest night,
Emerges a spark, a fragile light.
In the void, a heartbeat's sound,
The essence of life, profound.

With every echo, secrets dance,
In the abyss, I take a chance.
To hear the stories lost in time,
That weave the fabric of my rhyme.

In the stillness, the truth will rise,
Painting colors across the skies.
From the silent depths, I claim my song,
In this journey, I now belong.

Embracing the echoes of what was past,
A symphony born, forever to last.
In the abyss, I find my grace,
A tranquil heart, a sacred space.

Exploring the Depths of Stillness

In the quiet, shadows play,
Gentle whispers drift away.
Time, it seems, begins to pause,
Nature holds its breath, just because.

Ripples dance on the water's face,
Reflecting thoughts in this sacred space.
Birds call out, a soothing song,
Here in stillness, I belong.

Pebbles rest on the riverbed,
Stories told, yet never read.
Each moment, a canvas wide,
In the depths, I will confide.

The echoes of the world grow faint,
Silent prayers in the heart's quaint.
A journey deep beneath the skin,
Where all great wonders begin.

Lulled by the breeze, I stay still,
Each breath a promise, a silent thrill.
In this calm, I'm truly free,
Exploring depths inside of me.

An Odyssey Within the Heart

A voyage starts within the soul,
Mapping dreams, taking a toll.
With each pulse, a rhythm sings,
Unlocking treasures that the heart brings.

The mountains rise, daunting yet grand,
Footprints trace across the sand.
Whispers echo through the night,
Guiding me towards the light.

Through valleys deep, where shadows creep,
I gather strength from what I keep.
In silence, wisdom softly grows,
An inner journey only one knows.

Stars above begin to glow,
Their ancient tales, like rivers flow.
With every step, I find my way,
An odyssey that never sways.

In the chambers of my heart,
I awaken, and I restart.
Every beat, a chance to rise,
An adventure under endless skies.

Glimpses of Forgotten Realms

In the dusk, shadows amass,
Whispers of a time that has passed.
Through the curtains of the night,
Glimpses of realms come to light.

Echoes swirl in the cool air,
Faded tales, ancient and rare.
With each sigh, I travel far,
To landscapes kissed by the stars.

Broken bridges from the past,
Stories linger, shadows cast.
In the silence, memories gleam,
Threading the fabric of a dream.

Through forgotten doors I tread,
With a heart that's lightly led.
Magic hints at every turn,
In the depths, my spirit yearns.

With the dawn, I'll bring it near,
The essence of all I hold dear.
In the light, I seek to weave,
The stories that I once believed.

The Secret Depths of the Heart

In silent chambers, secrets dwell,
Whispers trapped in a hidden shell.
Each heartbeat, a tale untold,
In the depths, the brave unfold.

Beneath the surface, emotions stir,
A tapestry of quiet blur.
Through gentle waves of tranquil night,
The heart's shadows yearn for light.

Veiled in layers, they softly weave,
Stories of love and loss to cleave.
Within these walls, hope takes its flight,
Unraveling dreams in the soft twilight.

With every breath, the secrets sigh,
In the quiet, I learn to fly.
Through the depths, my spirit roams,
Finding solace in heart's homes.

The treasures found in pain and joy,
Each lesson crafted like a toy.
In the labyrinth of the heart's art,
I cherish the secret depths that I impart.

Voyage of the Heart's Compass

Set sail on waves of dreams,
With stars that guide our way,
Through storms and calmness gleams,
The heart's compass won't sway.

Each heartbeat is a voyage,
Every whisper, a refrain,
In the depths, we find courage,
Navigating love's terrain.

Hold tight to the anchor's pull,
As tides of change arise,
In the silence, hear it lull,
And watch the dawn greet skies.

Our sails are stitched with hope,
From fabric soft and bright,
With every swell, we cope,
Guided by the moonlight.

We journey with the night breeze,
Embracing what we learn,
In the voyage, find our peace,
And let the heart discern.

The Unwritten Story Within

Ink flows fresh on blank pages,
A tale waiting to unfold,
In the silence, life engages,
With whispers soft and bold.

Each heartbeat writes a chapter,
Where dreams and fears collide,
Among the joys and laughter,
The truth we cannot hide.

In shadows lurk the secrets,
Yet light can break the night,
The soul's dance, a duet,
Seeking its wings in flight.

With each breath, a reminder,
The story's still unclear,
But in the heart's reminder,
We find our way from here.

So pen your thoughts of wonder,
Let your voice guide the pen,
For in the storm, or thunder,
The tale will live again.

Beneath the Armor of the Soul

Beyond the shield we carry,
Lies softness we can't see,
Each scar and line a story,
Of battles fought, of being free.

In silence, hearts confide,
Where whispers weave the truth,
With every tear we hide,
Reflects the light of youth.

Armor may protect the dreamer,
Yet vulnerability's gold,
Find strength in being gentle,
In the warmth of being bold.

When shadows creep around,
And doubt begins to rise,
The soul can still be found,
Beneath the heavy sighs.

Peel back the layers, reveal,
The beauty that is you,
In the depths, we find what's real,
A light forever true.

Vistas of the Imagination

Through windows of the mind,
New worlds are born each day,
In colors yet defined,
Where dreams begin to play.

Mountains rise from thoughts anew,
Oceans whisper their song,
In every hue, in every view,
The heart knows it belongs.

Skylines dance with endless grace,
As hopes take flight and soar,
In this boundless, sacred space,
Imagination's door.

What stories leap from vision?
What wonders wait to grow?
In each heart's decision,
A spark ignites the glow.

So wander through your vistas wide,
Embrace each thought, each dream,
For in the mind's great tide,
Life flows like a stream.

The Subconscious Stream

In shadows deep where whispers play,
Thoughts like rivers drift away.
Tangled dreams and moments lost,
A journey taken, no matter the cost.

Beneath the surface, secrets flow,
In twilight's glow, they ebb and grow.
Visions dance in liquid light,
Guided by stars in the tranquil night.

Tides of memory wash ashore,
Echoes of love, longing, and more.
The stream of self, a fragile thread,
Weaving paths of the words unsaid.

In stillness found, the heart can hear,
Voices soft, both near and dear.
A current sways, a gentle pull,
As currents rise and moments lull.

Awake to dreams that softly gleam,
In the depths of the subconscious stream.
Flowing forth, let thoughts take flight,
In the quiet blooms the light.

Navigating the Currents of Identity

Among the waves where I reside,
The currents shift, a restless tide.
In mirrors deep, reflections sway,
I search for self in light and gray.

Guided by stars, the compass spins,
A quest for truth beneath my skin.
With every turn, each choice I make,
The currents swirl, rebirth or ache.

Caught in eddies of doubt and fear,
I navigate paths both strange and near.
Anchors weigh in currents strong,
Yet, I know my place, I belong.

In the tempest, I find my core,
Through stormy seas, I still explore.
With every ebb, a lesson learned,
In the tides of self, new fires burned.

I ride the waves, embrace the flow,
For every shadow helps me grow.
Navigating, I carve my way,
In this dance of night and day.

Beneath the Waves of Reflection

In quiet depths where secrets lie,
Ripples form, the past nearby.
Glimmers dance like fleeting light,
Beneath the waves, both dark and bright.

A mirror's edge, the thoughts unwind,
In shifting sands of heart and mind.
Every glance reveals the truth,
Fragments scattered, lost in youth.

I dive into the depths of me,
To find the voice that yearns to be.
Submerged in dreams, the shadows play,
Beneath the waves, night meets day.

Reflections whisper, tales untold,
Of wishes bright, and fears so bold.
I rise to surface with every breath,
Embracing life, in beauty, depth.

In tranquil waters, I seek to see,
What lies beneath, what sets me free.
Waves of reflection, soft and clear,
Reveal the self that I hold dear.

The Map of My Inner Cosmos

In starry realms where dreams align,
I chart the skies, my thoughts divine.
Each constellation tells a tale,
A journey vast, a daring sail.

Nebulas of wonder, vast and bright,
Guide my heart through the cosmic night.
Galaxies spin in swirling grace,
Mapping the contours of my space.

Planets dance in rhythmic flow,
Echoes of past, seeds I sow.
In quiet nights, I seek the signs,
The universe speaks in cosmic lines.

With every star, a piece of me,
I navigate to set me free.
Through space and time, my heart expands,
Writing my story with cosmic hands.

In this map of my inner skies,
I find the truth that never lies.
A journey vast, a path unfolds,
In the cosmos, my soul beholds.

Navigating the Soul's Depths

In murky waters, shadows play,
Whispers guide my fragile way.
Beneath the waves, secrets dwell,
In silent currents, truths to tell.

An anchor dropped in fathomless blue,
Each tug reveals a part of you.
With every rise, a surge of fears,
Yet depths hold solace, through the years.

A lighthouse shines on distant shores,
Illuminating forgotten doors.
The compass spins yet finds its course,
Through heart's dark depths, I seek the source.

Drifting softly, time has flown,
In these depths, I'm not alone.
The heartbeats echo, softly, loud,
As I navigate—a vessel proud.

Through tempests fierce and tranquil tides,
In the soul's depths, my spirit abides.
Finding strength in every part,
This journey leads me to my heart.

Echoes of the Mind's Sea

Waves of thought crash on the shore,
Whispers linger, seeking more.
In the silence, echoes dance,
Caught in a sweet, fleeting trance.

Each tide brings a memory clear,
Lapping at the edges near.
In depths unseen, emotions swell,
As stories weave, they start to tell.

The currents pull, they twist, they turn,
In the quiet, old fires burn.
Mist on the horizon's line,
Signals lost in skies divine.

Dancing ripples, a tale unfolds,
Within the mind's sea, forever holds.
Navigating through its vast expanse,
I find the courage to take a chance.

With each wave, a lesson learned,
In the depths, my heart has yearned.
The mind's sea flows, it ebbs and breaks,
In its embrace, my spirit wakes.

Journey Within the Silent Chambers

In chambers deep, silence reigns,
Echoes linger, joy and pains.
Each step forward, a whispered call,
Guiding me through shadowed hall.

Ancient walls holding my fears,
Time's embrace muffles my tears.
Yet in the stillness, hope ignites,
Illuminating solitary nights.

A door ajar, a glimpse of light,
Leads me on, through darkest night.
Fragments of laughter, soft and clear,
Remind me of the love held dear.

As I wander through thought's maze,
I find strength in gentle praise.
These silent chambers, rich with grace,
Reflect the depths of my embrace.

Understanding blooms where silence thrives,
In hidden corners, memory lives.
My journey within breathes new dawn,
In silent chambers, I am reborn.

Odyssey of the Heart's Reflection

In the mirrors of soul's design,
Reflections shift, both yours and mine.
An odyssey through love's embrace,
Searching for the hidden trace.

Each glimmer speaks of dreams once lost,\nNavigating
through love's cost.
Vows written in stars above,
Woven tightly, threads of love.

Beneath the surface, currents flow,
In depths of feeling, we both know.
An endless journey, path entwined,
In heart's reflection, souls aligned.

Through storms that rattle, still we stay,
With every heartbeat, come what may.
The odyssey guides us from afar,
Illuminated by hope's bright star.

Together we face what time may yield,
In the heart's reflection, truth revealed.
An endless sea, both wild and vast,
In this odyssey, we find our past.

The Winding Path of Introspection

In shadows deep, I wander slow,
Through silent whispers, thoughts do flow.
Each turn reveals a subtle truth,
The heart's own map, the light of youth.

With every step, a question grows,
In mirrored lakes, the stillness shows.
What lies within, a maze of dreams,
Or flickering hopes in silver beams?

The echoes call from distant lands,
As fingers trace the shifting sands.
Reflection pools in quiet streams,
The mind embraced by tender themes.

A journey wrought with hints of light,
Through darkest hours into the bright.
Each breath a scent of aged resolve,
In labyrinths where souls evolve.

With courage as my guiding star,
I seek the truths my heart's aware.
The path unwinds, yet leads me home,
In introspection, I freely roam.

Beneath the Surface of Thought

In waters deep, the thoughts reside,
Beneath the calm, where secrets hide.
Each ripple stirs the depths anew,
As currents pull, my senses skew.

Tangled roots of memories bind,
Reaching for light, so hard to find.
A world uncharted, strange and vast,
Where whispers linger, shadows cast.

The surface sways with fleeting grace,
Yet deep inside, a hidden place.
Where reason flows like ancient streams,
And clarity reveals the seams.

Through depths of doubt, I dive and swim,
To chase the light, to find within.
A treasure trove of thought unspooled,
Where silence reigns and fears are cooled.

Each journey taught by tides of time,
Emerging waves, a silent rhyme.
Beneath the surface, life awaits,
With gentle truths that love creates.

Secrets of the Unseen Voyage

A ship sets sail on whispers low,
Across the skies, where wild winds blow.
Each wave a secret, deep and old,
In heart's embrace, the dreams unfold.

The stars align, a map in night,
With every turn, a chance for light.
To drift in silence, eyes wide shut,
Transform the dark into a gut.

What lies beyond the veil of sight,
In realms where shadows dance with light?
An unseen voyage calls my name,
Through currents wild, igniting flame.

The pulse of time, a gentle wave,
Each heartbeat echoes, strong and brave.
In depths unexplored, I seek my fate,
A treasure's glow, I navigate.

The mysteries of the night enfold,
As stories weave, and stars turn gold.
Secrets linger in every breath,
In unseen waves, outwitting death.

Tides of the Spirit's Current

Each tide a whisper, soft and true,
Carving paths that bend anew.
The spirit's dance in fluid grace,
Reflects the soul's own sacred space.

In moonlit pull, the heart does sway,
To ebb and flow, to dream and play.
With salty air, the essence swirls,
A symphony of light unfurls.

The ocean's vast, a timeless flow,
Where every drop can learn and grow.
Embracing change, the waves collide,
In surf and foam, the spirits ride.

Awash in colors, bright and bold,
The current draws, like tales of old.
In quiet moments, truth designed,
With tides of spirit, hearts aligned.

As every wave returns, it sings,
Of deeper dreams and fervent things.
The endless flow, a dance of grace,
In tides of spirit, I find my place.

Chasing the Echoes Within

In shadows deep where whispers stir,
A memory calls, a gentle blur.
With every breath, a sound we trace,
Chasing echoes in this quiet space.

Through winding paths our thoughts will roam,
In search of truths that we call home.
Each heartbeat drifts like waves on sand,
Echoes guide us, hand in hand.

Beyond the veil where secrets lie,
We find our hopes, we learn to fly.
With open hearts, we seek the light,
Chasing echoes through the night.

In every sigh, a story sings,
Of lost tomorrows and yearning springs.
The past a song that softly weaves,
The echoes whisper what one believes.

So step with grace, embrace the sound,
In echoes lost, new dreams are found.
Through silent calls, we break the chains,
Chasing echoes, shedding pains.

The Heart's Secret Pathways

In quiet corners, a path unseen,
The heart reveals what lies in between.
Whispers of love and dreams untold,
A journey through memories, both warm and cold.

Each heartbeat dances, a tale to share,
Tracing the lines of hope and despair.
Through winding roads, we learn and grow,
Unlocking doors where feelings flow.

The heart speaks softly, a gentle guide,
Through secret pathways, side by side.
With every turn, a lesson learned,
In whispers of love, passions burned.

In shadows deep, the truth will rise,
A journey forged beneath the skies.
With heartbeats echoing strong and clear,
The secret pathways reveal our fear.

So walk the trails, embrace the fire,
In heart's pathways, we find desire.
Through every choice, we're led anew,
The heart's secret, a sacred view.

The Hidden Map of Self-Discovery

In pages worn, the map unfolds,
A journey written in stories told.
With every line, we seek the truth,
A hidden path, the essence of youth.

Through valleys deep and mountains high,
The map reveals where dreams can fly.
Each step we take, a choice to make,
Tracing the lines, we bend, we break.

With every mystery, a lesson shown,
The hidden map, a heart of stone.
In timeless whispers, wisdom flows,
Through broken trails, the spirit grows.

The compass turns, a gentle nudge,
To find our way, we must not judge.
In every scar, a truth to seek,
The hidden map of the humble and meek.

So forge ahead with open hands,
In self-discovery, the heart expands.
Through every journey, souls ignite,
The hidden map reveals our light.

Ripples of Past and Present

In the stillness, ripples flow,
Carrying tales of long ago.
The past, a whisper, faint but near,
In every moment, we hold dear.

From echoes formed in time's embrace,
We learn to dance with every trace.
Ripples spread from heart to heart,
Uniting stories that never part.

The present sings with vibrant hues,
In every choice, the past renews.
With every glance, a thread unwinds,
Ripples shimmer, where fate binds.

In the dance of time, we intertwine,
Past and present, a sacred line.
With open hearts, let memories weave,
Ripples of love, we dare believe.

So cast your stones into the sea,
Embrace the ripples wild and free.
In every heartbeat, life transcends,
Ripples of past and present blend.

Maps of the Forgotten Heart

In shadows where memories dwell,
Old maps lie to tell their tale.
Each crease holds a silent spell,
Worn edges whisper of the frail.

Lost paths carved in time's embrace,
Footsteps fading, lost in dust.
A heart once bold, now a trace,
In longing's grip, we place our trust.

The ink bleeds soft with every sigh,
Ink-stained with tears not shed.
Dreams entwined like branches high,
Reaching for what's long since fled.

Veins of love run deep and wide,
Yet maps grow dim, their use decays.
What once was home now is denied,
A journey through forgotten ways.

But in the folds, a glimmer glows,
A compass in the silent dark.
To navigate the heart that knows,
The warmth of love, the light, the spark.

Whispers in the Labyrinth of Mind

In corridors of thought we tread,
Echoes murmur, soft and low.
Each turn reveals what's left unsaid,
Patterns lost in ebb and flow.

A candle flickers, shadows dance,
Illuminating fears concealed.
Thoughts entwined in a fleeting trance,
Secrets of the heart revealed.

In tangled threads, confusion swells,
Silent cries for clarity.
A symphony of muted bells,
Resonance of disparity.

Yet through the maze, a voice calls loud,
A truth hidden behind the veil.
Guiding souls amidst the crowd,
On wings of hope, they gently sail.

Through every twist, we seek the light,
In darkened realms where doubts reside.
Whispers echo, pierce the night,
In labyrinths where minds collide.

Sailing on the Sea of Reflection

Beneath a sky painted in blue,
The waves whisper tales of old.
With every crest, a thought anew,
Seas of dreams and stories told.

A vessel made of fragile wood,
Guided by the stars above.
In quiet moments, we find good,
Navigating with gentle love.

Each ripple carries whispers soft,
Of choices made and paths not crossed.
Winds of change push dreams aloft,
In stillness, we find what was lost.

Reflections shimmer on the tide,
Echoing depths within the soul.
In every wave, our hearts abide,
Searching for what makes us whole.

As the horizon beckons near,
New journeys wait in golden light.
We sail on oceans, void of fear,
In the embrace of day and night.

The Tides of Introspection

When the world falls silent, we dive deep,
Into the waters of our thoughts.
The calm reveals what we must keep,
And sheds the weight of all that's fraught.

Each ripple holds a fleeting truth,
A glimpse of what we often veil.
In reflections, we find our youth,
A mirror where our dreams prevail.

The ebb and flow of heartbeats hum,
Resonating with inner peace.
In solitude, we quietly come,
To understand and release.

The tides may pull, yet also guide,
The journey inward is a quest.
In every wave, we find a side,
Of ourselves that longs for rest.

As dusk descends, we softly sigh,
Content with what the mind unfolds.
The heart learns how to let love fly,
Through introspection, it grows bold.

Streams of Silence and Solitude

In quiet woods, the shadows fall,
Whispers of night, a soft enthrall.
The gentle breeze, a soothing sigh,
Where secrets linger, time drifts by.

A brook meanders, clear and bright,
Reflecting stars, a velvety night.
Each ripple tells a tale untold,
In solitude, my heart grows bold.

The moonlight dances on the trees,
Carried softly on the breeze.
In silence deep, I find my way,
With dreams that hush the break of day.

As echoes fade into the past,
In solitude, I find the vast.
These streams of thought, so pure and clear,
Guide me through the paths I steer.

In every pause, a world unfolds,
In quiet moments, my spirit holds.
No need for voices loud and wild,
In silence, I am nature's child.

The Tapestry of Dreams and Desires

Threads of hope weave the night,
With each color, a bold new light.
Dreams intertwine, a dance begun,
In the fabric, our lives are spun.

Scarlet wishes, azure sighs,
Embroidered tales beneath the skies.
Every stitch, a heart's delight,
Telling stories of love's flight.

Golden ambitions, silver fears,
Knit together through laughter and tears.
In the loom of fate, we find our place,
A tapestry shaped with gentle grace.

From whispers soft to shouts so grand,
The threads connect, hand in hand.
With every pattern, a desire grows,
In this woven world, our spirit flows.

So let us create, with hearts ablaze,
A tapestry bright, through all our days.
In the dance of dreams, let us aspire,
To light the world with endless fire.

Serenity in the Depths Below

Beneath the waves, a world so still,
Where time drifts softly, like a quill.
In coral gardens, peace abides,
A sanctuary where calm resides.

The ocean hums a lullaby,
With every tide, it swells and sighs.
In blue embrace, the soul can dive,
In depths unknown, the heart's alive.

A silent dance with shadows near,
Where light and dark combine, sincere.
Every bubble, a thought set free,
In serenity, the spirit sees.

The currents whisper ancient lore,
In quietude, we're free to explore.
The ocean's heart, a mirror deep,
In its embrace, our dreams can sleep.

So drift along, in tranquil flows,
Embrace the calm that nature shows.
In depths below, find peace anew,
In every wave, life starts anew.

The Hidden Compass of Thought

In twilight hours, the mind will roam,
Through valleys deep, it finds a home.
With every query, paths unfold,
A compass hidden, truth be told.

Each thought a star in night's embrace,
Guiding journeys, setting pace.
In quiet moments, insights gleam,
The heart knows well, the mind can dream.

Maps are drawn in silent spheres,
Crafted gently from hopes and fears.
With wisdom's light, we break the ground,
In every doubt, our strength is found.

The compass spins, both wild and keen,
Through every struggle, yet unseen.
In labyrinths of thought, we chart,
The hidden paths that reach the heart.

So navigate this inner tide,
With courage bold, let love be your guide.
In every turn, let truth be sought,
Embrace the journey, treasure thought.

The Soul's Afloat in Silent Waters

Drifting softly, calm and free,
In the depths of serenity.
A whisper stirs the echoed light,
Guiding dreams through the night.

Ripples dance upon the face,
Each is touched by gentle grace.
Beneath the stars, a tranquil plea,
Embracing all that's meant to be.

Thoughts like feathers softly fall,
Floating free, they heed the call.
In the silence, solace found,
The heart's soft rhythm, a sacred sound.

Mirrored depths where secrets sleep,
In this stillness, feelings creep.
Awake within the water's flow,
Lit by the moon, their essence glow.

A journey through the silent sea,
Unraveled thoughts, a memory.
The soul awaits the dawn's embrace,
Drifting on in timeless space.

Beneath the Veil of Consciousness

Shadows dance in the afterthought,
Hidden truths in battles fought.
Waves of silence crash in mind,
Seeking what is left behind.

Veils of doubt cloud every dream,
Yet flickers glow, a hopeful beam.
Threads of wisdom softly weave,
In stillness, we learn to believe.

Echoes swirl in the twilight,
Whispers hint at inner light.
Through the guise of what is known,
Awakening seeds we have sown.

In the depths, reflections play,
Carving paths through the gray.
A journey inward, step by step,
Unveiling layers we have kept.

Emerging from the quiet night,
With every breath, we find our sight.
Beneath the veil, we reconnect,
In consciousness, our hearts reflect.

Room for Reflection

Within these walls, the heart unfolds,
In every shadow, a story told.
Memories flicker like candlelight,
Illuminating the edges of night.

Mirrored surfaces reveal the soul,
A sanctuary, a space to stroll.
Thoughts meander, soft and slow,
In this haven, the mind can grow.

Whispers linger in the air,
Softly urging me to care.
Time slows down, and I can see,
The hidden paths that set me free.

Each corner cradles dreams untold,
An echo of the brave and bold.
In this room of silent grace,
I find my heart, a sacred place.

Reflection deepens as shadows blend,
In solitude, my spirit mends.
Nestled here, I breathe, I find,
A room for wonder, heart, and mind.

The Mirror of Inner Space

Across the void, a whisper calls,
In the mirror, the spirit sprawls.
Flickering visions, endless sights,
Glimpses of truths, a dance of lights.

This inner space, a vast expanse,
Where thoughts awaken and dreams dance.
Reflections shift through layers deep,
Guarding the secrets that we keep.

Each echo tells a tale profound,
In silence, the answers abound.
With every gaze, I delve within,
To uncover the places I've been.

The mirror holds a sacred key,
Unlocking who I'm meant to be.
In this realm, I learn to soar,
Finding joy on unseen shores.

Through every ripple, I can see,
A glimpse of what is yet to be.
In the mirror of this inner space,
I weave my dreams, embrace my grace.

Wandering in the Landscape of Dreams

In twilight's glow, I drift along,
Soft echoes of a distant song.
Mountains rise where shadows play,
And stars awaken night from day.

A river flows with silver light,
Whispers dance in gentle night.
I chase the clouds, I follow streams,
In this vast world of floating dreams.

Paths unfold where secrets lie,
Barefoot on the starlit sky.
Each step a chance, a door to fate,
In vivid realms, I meditate.

Colors swirl, the air is sweet,
In visions bold, our hearts will meet.
Time dissolves, I'm free to roam,
In this enchanted place called home.

With every breath, I'm further lost,
Yet find a truth, no matter the cost.
In wandering light, I find my way,
In this landscape where dreams will stay.

Labyrinths of the Inner World

In winding paths, the shadows weave,
Each turn a thought, each pause, believe.
Mirrors gleam with hidden faces,
Reflecting deep, forgotten places.

A whisper here, a secret shared,
In tangled dreams, the heart laid bare.
I trace the lines of fears and grace,
In every corner, I seek my place.

Labyrinths twist, the mind's a maze,
Lost in wonder, lost in haze.
Yet within the chaos, light breaks through,
Revealing paths to what is true.

Steps echo soft on ancient stone,
In silence found, I'm never alone.
Each darkened turn, each fleeting sight,
Guides me closer to my light.

In this journey, I learn to trust,
The labyrinth's soul becomes a must.
With courage firm, I face what's stored,
In every wound, there's love restored.

Whispers from a Hidden Well

Deep within the earth so still,
Lies the heart of a secret well.
Echoes call from depths unknown,
In silence where the truth is sown.

A gentle voice, a soft refrain,
Dancing lightly, touching pain.
I lean to hear the stories past,
In every sigh, a spell is cast.

Water glimmers, cool and clear,
In its depths, I face my fear.
The whispers guide, they lead me down,
Unraveling threads of the crown.

From ancient roots, wisdom flows,
In every drop, the spirit grows.
The hidden well, a mirror true,
Reflects the dreams that once I knew.

With every drop, the waters blend,
In this embrace, I start to mend.
Secrets cherished, shadows lift,
In this calm, I find my gift.

Exploring the Shadows of the Self

In the stillness, shadows breathe,
Each hidden part I softly weave.
I journey deep, where few dare go,
To meet the self I yearn to know.

Patterns dance in muted light,
Reflections shimmer, dark and bright.
With open heart, I face the night,
In every fear, a spark ignites.

Fragments lost, so much to gain,
In the mirror, I feel the pain.
Yet through the dark, I'm learning grace,
Accepting all, I find my place.

Voices rise from deep within,
Embracing truth, I shed my skin.
Each shadow holds a story told,
In every tale, a flame of gold.

Unraveled now, I'm free to be,
In shadows cast, I find the key.
Exploring depths, I claim my soul,
In this journey, I am whole.

Treasury of the Inner Landscape

In valleys deep where shadows play,
The whispers of the heart will sway.
Beneath the stars, our dreams arise,
Gold hidden softly in moonlit skies.

A tapestry of thoughts unfolds,
With threads of silver, bright and bold.
Each moment crafted, time entwined,
A treasure trove within the mind.

Through streams of consciousness, we roam,
Foundations laid, we build our home.
On hills of wonder, peaks of thought,
A landscape rich with lessons taught.

In stillness found, the world retreats,
Where echoes dance in rhythmic beats.
In nature's arms, the soul takes flight,
A treasury of pure delight.

We harvest light from shadows cast,
Transforming dreams, we're free at last.
The inner world, a sacred space,
A vibrant realm of time and grace.

Illuminating the Unconscious

In corridors of dreams, we dwell,
Where secrets linger and stories tell.
Flickers bright, like stars, they glow,
Revealing paths we do not know.

With gentle brush, we paint the night,
Unraveling fears, embracing light.
Each thought a star, a guiding fire,
Illuminating deep desire.

Through shadowed halls of mind we tread,
Awakening echoes of the dead.
In silence, whispers softly rise,
Unconscious truths in velvet skies.

Each moment holds a hidden spark,
In darkest corners, we embark.
A journey through, we dare to seek,
The depths of self, the strong, the weak.

In clarity, our visions churn,
To seek the lessons we must learn.
Illuminated hearts will sing,
In realms where dreams and fears take wing.

Solitary Shores of the Mind

Upon the sands where silence breathes,
The ocean's edge, a truth it weaves.
Waves crashing soft, a lullaby,
Solitude whispers, letting time fly.

Each grain a thought, each tide a change,
In quiet corners, worlds arrange.
The horizon calls in shades of blue,
A canvas stretched where dreams come true.

With every breeze, old memories sway,
Casting away the weight of day.
In solitude's embrace, we find,
The shores of peace within the mind.

Footprints fade where thoughts collide,
In tranquil moments, we confide.
As dusk descends and shadows play,
The mind's retreat at end of day.

On solitary shores we stand,
Embracing life, both wild and bland.
In quiet depths, our spirits soar,
On waves of thought, forever more.

Reflections from a Hidden Ocean

Beneath the surface, currents flow,
In hidden depths, our truths bestow.
Mirrors dance with visions bright,
Reflections caught in soft twilight.

Each ripple holds a tale untold,
In whispers of the brave and bold.
An ocean deep of heart's desire,
Where dreams ignite and souls conspire.

In tranquil waters, shadows glide,
As hidden fears we will not hide.
With echoes of the past in sight,
We navigate the dark, then light.

A voyage through the soul's expanse,
Embracing fate with every chance.
An ocean vast, so rich, so wide,
Where Love and Loss must coincide.

So dive into this hidden sea,
Where each reflection sets us free.
In every wave, a part of us,
The depths reveal in peace and trust.

Charting the Hidden Currents

In the depths where silence grows,
Secrets swim where no one goes.
Whispers drift on twilight's sigh,
Mapping paths beneath the sky.

Beneath the waves, a story sways,
Hidden truths in gentle plays.
Currents pull with subtle grace,
Leading dreams to shadowed place.

Glimmers flash as stars ignite,
Guiding souls through endless night.
Every turn, a mystery spun,
Lessons learned, yet never done.

Depths reveal what hearts conceal,
True reflections start to peel.
With every splash a tale unfolds,
A treasure waiting to be told.

Charting journeys through the deep,
In the silence, secrets keep.
Following the currents' dance,
Finding hope, and lost romance.

Odyssey into the Starlit Dreamscape

Beneath a sky of diamond light,
Wanderers tread on dreams at night.
Each twinkling star, a beacon bright,
Guiding hearts in fearless flight.

In the hush where wishes weave,
Stories breathe and softly leave.
Shadows long and whispers near,
Echo dreams, dissolve our fear.

Galaxies in swirling dance,
Holding time in gentle trance.
Through the cosmos, drift we must,
In the stardust, find our trust.

With every step, we seek and yearn,
Lessons from the night we learn.
A voyage through the vast, unknown,
In starlit realms, we find our home.

Odyssey of heart and mind,
In the depths, our peace we find.
Woven paths of light and dream,
In the starlit night, we beam.

A Pilgrimage of Shadows

Through the twilight, figures roam,
Each step leads us far from home.
Whispers echo, a haunting song,
In the night where souls belong.

Footsteps trace a sacred ground,
In the silence, truth is found.
Shadows dance and linger near,
Guiding pathways from our fear.

Flickers of the past awake,
Marking journeys we must take.
Memories rise as shadows play,
Lighting paths along the way.

Veils of night begin to lift,
In our hearts, the shadows sift.
Finding strength in what we've lost,
Embracing dreams at any cost.

A pilgrimage through time and space,
Every shadow leaves its trace.
Within the dark, we find the light,
In shadows deep, we navigate night.

The Current of Unspoken Thoughts

In the stillness where we linger,
Thoughts unvoiced slip through our fingers.
A current flows beneath the skin,
Silent echoes from within.

Words unsaid, a heavy tide,
Carrying dreams that we must hide.
In the shadows, whispers crawl,
Yearning to break the silent wall.

Beneath the surface, feelings churn,
Yearning hearts, for love they yearn.
Navigating currents deep and wide,
Hopes and fears we cannot hide.

In the dance of thoughts unshared,
Silent burdens, hearts laid bare.
Flowing through this quiet stream,
Searching for a voice to dream.

The currents pull with gentle might,
Guiding us through endless night.
In the silence, we shall find,
A way to heal the heart and mind.

Mapping the Internals

In silent chambers, thoughts collide,
Whispers echo, secrets hide.
Each corner holds a tale untold,
Dreams interwoven, threads of gold.

Paths diverge in maze-like grace,
Memories linger in empty space.
A map of feelings, rich and deep,
In shadows where the heart does leap.

Light flickers on forgotten doors,
Buried hopes and ancient scores.
Each breath unveils a hidden truth,
The soul reborn, eternally soothed.

Rivers of thought start to flow,
Winding where no one can go.
Navigating through the unseen,
Finding solace where I've been.

A compass made of dreams and fears,
Charting fate through laughter and tears.
With every heartbeat, I redefine,
My spirit's map, forever mine.

A Journey Within the Mind's Eye

In twilight's glow, the journey starts,
A realm where silence fills the parts.
Through corridors of endless night,
I wander under starry light.

Visions bloom like petals rare,
Floating dreams hang in the air.
With each breath, the past unfolds,
Whispers of wisdom, stories of old.

A tapestry of thought takes shape,
Patterns emerge from an unseen drape.
In shadows deep, I find the spark,
Illuminating the profound dark.

Moments flicker, like candle's flame,
Every echo calls my name.
A swirling dance of time and space,
The mind's eye reveals its grace.

With courage, I traverse the maze,
Unfolding truths in myriad ways.
A journey where the heart beats strong,
Uniting me with the cosmos' song.

Cerulean Dreams Beneath

Beneath the waves of deep cerulean,
Lies a world, unknown, yet still within.
Dreams drift softly, like tides that flow,
Painting stories where the heart can glow.

Each ripple carries a whisper sweet,
Secret tales of love and defeat.
Bubbles rise with hopes untold,
Unraveling moments, cherished gold.

Skeletons of starfish lie asleep,
Guardians of secrets, shadows deep.
Embracing the quiet, where silence reigns,
Tracing the lines of joy and pains.

Coral reefs sing of vibrant life,
A dance of color, joy, and strife.
In waters clear, reflections gleam,
Holding the weight of every dream.

The ocean hums a lullaby,
Cradled gently, we drift and fly.
In cerulean depths, I dive and seek,
The hope and magic— soft and unique.

The Inner Cosmos Unfurled

Within the depths of soul's expanse,
Galaxies swirl in a cosmic dance.
Stars ignite in whispered prayers,
Mapping existence with cosmic layers.

Nebulae weave through darkened skies,
Illuminating where the spirit lies.
Each twinkle births a secret thrill,
In silence where the mind stands still.

Planets orbit feelings vast,
Bonding futures with echoes of past.
Gravity pulls at the heart's design,
Tethering dreams in a celestial line.

Supernovae of joy explode,
Lighting paths that wisdom showed.
Cosmic winds whisper through the night,
Guiding lost souls to the light.

In this universe, we learn to soar,
Finding balance on the cosmic floor.
Embracing each moment, bright and unfurled,
We dance together in this inner world.

The Veil of Quiet Reflections

In stillness deep, the shadows dance,
Whispers echo, lost in trance.
A mirror holds the secrets told,
In silver light, the past unfolds.

Like petals soft in twilight's grip,
The heart's embrace, a gentle slip.
Each thought a leaf on water's face,
Flowing softly, finding grace.

Beneath the veil, the truths abide,
In quiet corners, thoughts collide.
Moments linger, softly spun,
Where time and dreams are gently one.

The night sky calls with stars aglow,
As deep reflections shimmer slow.
In hushed tones, the world breathes in,
A sacred space where love begins.

With every breath, the echoes rise,
The promises beneath the skies.
In gentle waves, our souls unite,
In the veil of quiet, we find light.

Scales of the Inner Ocean

Beneath the surface, a world awaits,
Waves of thought that twist and shape.
Scales glimmer in shades unknown,
In this deep sea, we find our home.

Currents pull, the tides they sing,
Of silent sorrows and hope's bright wing.
In depths so dark, the silence reigns,
Yet whispers rise from hidden pains.

The mind's ocean, vast and wide,
A vessel born from dreams inside.
In every swell, a story flows,
In every crest, the truth bestows.

Upon the shore, the heart will tread,
With every step, new paths are spread.
The calm and storm, a dance profound,
In scales of blue, our souls are found.

As stars reflect upon the tide,
In this inner sea, we confide.
Embrace the waves, let go of fear,
In the depths, the light is clear.

Rhythms of the Heart's Solitude

In the quiet space where shadows dwell,
A heartbeat speaks, a silent bell.
Echoes ring in chambers deep,
Where solitude and solace weep.

The ticking clock, a gentle guide,
Amidst the whispers, thoughts reside.
In the rhythm, a pulse of night,
Loneliness held in tender light.

When silence wraps the world in blue,
The heart knows well what is true.
With every sigh, a soft refrain,
In solitude, we learn of pain.

Yet within the hush, a spark ignites,
Each quiet moment, a chance for flight.
In stillness found, the spirit grows,
In the heart's solitude, love flows.

Dancing softly with the stars above,
In the rhythm lies a hidden love.
An echo fades, yet memories stay,
In solitude's arms, we find our way.

Through the Looking Glass of Dreams

A wondrous realm behind the glass,
Where shadows blend and specters pass.
Through veils of mist, the moments soar,
Each dream a key to an open door.

Reflections twist in colors bright,
Worlds unfold in pure delight.
In whispered scenes, the heart finds peace,
In dreams' embrace, our fears release.

The mirror sings a song untold,
Of stories cast in silver bold.
In lucid dance, we drift away,
Through corridors where spirits play.

Each glance reveals a deeper truth,
Unraveling the threads of youth.
In the looking glass, we find our voice,
In whispered dreams, we make our choice.

With every blink, the worlds converge,
In dream's embrace, our souls emerge.
Through the glass, we wander free,
In the tapestry of what will be.

Beneath the Echoing Skies

Beneath the echoing skies,
The whispers of the night,
Stars twinkle in disguise,
Guiding hearts to the light.

Gentle winds weave their song,
A melody soft and sweet,
Carried where dreams belong,
In the shadows, they meet.

Clouds drift like fleeting thoughts,
Chasing the moon's silver glow,
In the silence, hope is sought,
Where only dreamers go.

Time dances on the edge,
Painting tales with each breath,
In the twilight's soft hedge,
Life and love conquer death.

Beneath the echoing skies,
Eternity finds its place,
With the stars as our ties,
In this vast, boundless space.

Compass of the Unseen

In the compass of the unseen,
Where shadows softly glide,
Timeless truths lie between,
The worlds both dark and wide.

Navigating through the night,
With hearts as our true guide,
Each step illuminated bright,
By faith, we will abide.

Secrets whispered on the breeze,
Carried far from the past,
Guiding us with gentle ease,
Towards futures unsurpassed.

The stars map our silent way,
While the moon watches near,
In this dance of night and day,
We seek what we hold dear.

With the compass set to roam,
We journey, hand in hand,
In the unseen, we find home,
Together we will stand.

The Unraveled Threads of Self

The unraveled threads of self,
Lay scattered to the wind,
Each knot a borrowed wealth,
Of stories lost and pinned.

Woven in the fabric's grain,
Are colors bright and true,
In joy and sorrow's stain,
We find the shades of you.

Every twist speaks of a stain,
Of love, of loss, of grace,
In the tapestry, our pain,
Finds beauty in its place.

As the loom spins endlessly,
We gather what we weave,
In the dance of memory,
We learn how to believe.

Through threads both weak and strong,
A portrait starts to rise,
In the fabric, we belong,
Stitched beneath endless skies.

Echoing Footsteps in the Void

Echoing footsteps in the void,
Sound of silence profound,
Every moment, joy or dread,
Leaves a mark without a sound.

In the stillness, shadows play,
Guiding paths we must take,
Where memories lead the way,
In the depths, we awake.

Footprints etched in soft despair,
Fade with the morning light,
Yet within the stillness there,
Lies a spark, warm and bright.

Voices whisper from afar,
As the heart starts to soar,
In the quiet, we are stars,
Shining forevermore.

Echoing footsteps stir the night,
In the maze of our mind,
Through the dark, we search for light,
In the void, ourselves, we find.

Driftwood from the Heart's Journey

Washed ashore on sandy strands,
Echoes linger in grainy hands.
Time carves tales upon the wood,
Words unsaid, yet understood.

Each wave whispers, a soft refrain,
Stories of joy, sorrow, and pain.
Driftwood scattered, lost yet found,
Hearts connect in silence profound.

In the current of life's embrace,
We seek solace, a sacred space.
Fragments of love, hopes that we weave,
In every shard, we dare believe.

Weathered lines like paths we tread,
Memories etched, the tears we shed.
Nature's canvas, rough yet fair,
A testament to the hearts that care.

As twilight falls, the sky aglow,
Each piece of driftwood tells what we know.
Together they dance, a silent art,
A journey traced from the heart.

Uncharted Depths of Emotion

Beneath the surface, waters churn,
Secrets await, the depths we yearn.
Ripples of laughter, cries of despair,
Uncharted realms we all must dare.

Instincts pull like tides at night,
Navigating shadows, seeking light.
The ocean swells with whispers clear,
Each wave echoing what we fear.

Veins run deep with stories untold,
Hearts like anchors, steadfast and bold.
A voyage through the churn and swell,
Each heartbeat a tale, a truth to tell.

Waves crash gently upon the shore,
Creating spaces to explore.
With every surge, our spirits rise,
In the depths, we find our ties.

Cast away doubts, let currents steer,
Embrace the chaos, face the fear.
The sea of feeling, vast and wild,
Awaits the brave, the unbeguiled.

Sailing in the Sea of Memory

With every gust, the sails take flight,
Across the waves, beneath starlight.
Memories glimmer like distant stars,
Guiding the way through night's avatars.

The whispers of past summers' glow,
Echo in waves, they ebb and flow.
Drifting through time, the heart feels bold,
Stories unfold, like sails of gold.

In tranquil moments, tempest roars,
Each heartbeat a knock upon old doors.
Recollections dance in the moon's embrace,
Bringing warmth to this sacred space.

The sea remembers, tides hold fast,
Lessons learned from journeys past.
Every current, every breeze,
Carries the weight of memories' ease.

Through storms or stillness, we find our way,
Sailing onward into the day.
Each wave a burst of laughter shared,
In the sea of memory, love declared.

Meditations on the Misty Waters

In the stillness, the fog draws near,
Veiling the landscape, soft and clear.
Thoughts drift like boats, gently sway,
A medley of dreams lost in the gray.

Ripples of silence, echoes of time,
Each breath a prayer, a sacred rhyme.
Misty waters, calming and deep,
Harbor the secrets we wish to keep.

Beyond the veil, whispers collide,
In shadows where secrets abide.
Reflections shimmer, memories blend,
In this space, we mend and transcend.

With each moment, the stillness grows,
In quiet depths, the heart overflows.
Meditations on water, soft and light,
Guide us gently through the night.

In the mist's embrace, we find retreat,
A path to solace, timeless and sweet.
As fog lifts, we greet the dawn,
In the quiet hours, love reborn.

A Quest Beyond the Known

In shadows deep, we dare to tread,
With stars above, our hopes are fed.
Through valleys vast and mountains tall,
We seek the truth that beckons all.

The map unfolds with every day,
In whispers soft, the signs convey.
Each step we take, a tale untold,
A treasure found, more precious than gold.

With every dawn, the light will show,
The paths we've paved, the dreams we sow.
In courage bold, our spirits soar,
To realms unknown, we yearn for more.

The winds will guide, the rivers flow,
As we embrace what lies below.
With open hearts, we strive to feel,
The quest itself, our greatest seal.

In company with souls we meet,
Together strong, we stand on feet.
The journey shared—a bond so bright,
Beyond the known, we find our light.

The Mirage of the Self

In mirrors cold, reflections play,
The self we see, so far away.
In foggy realms of doubt and fear,
The truths we seek, they disappear.

A phantom dance, the ego sways,
In tangled webs, we lose our ways.
Yet deep within, a spark remains,
A whispered voice that calls our names.

Through shifting sands and fleeting days,
We search for meaning, caught in maze.
What lies beneath the skin we wear?
A hidden depth, a truth laid bare.

With open mind, we question fate,
The heart's embrace, it won't await.
In solitude, we face the storm,
To find the self—a new reborn.

In stillness find the quiet breath,
The mirage fades, revealing depth.
Embrace the journey, feel the whole,
For in the quest, we find our soul.

Unraveling the Threads of Being

In tapestry of life we weave,
Each thread connects, we must believe.
With every twist, a story spun,
In colors bright, or shadows run.

The past and future, intertwined,
A legacy in hearts, aligned.
Through trials faced and joys we share,
We gather strength, we learn to care.

Within the fabric, patterns show,
The paths we've walked, the love we know.
Each thread a lesson, rich and bold,
In silence kept, a truth unfolds.

As needles clash, the fabric sings,
A symphony of sacred things.
In every stitch, a tale of grace,
In life's embrace, we find our place.

So weave with courage, heart ablaze,
Through every storm, through sunlit days.
For in the threads, a life is found,
In unity, our hearts are bound.

Parallel Journeys of the Heart

Two hearts that beat, yet walk alone,
In whispered dreams, the seeds are sown.
A dance of fate, with paths that part,
Yet pull us close, entwined in art.

In secret glances, stories bloom,
Through silent nights, we sense the room.
The resonance of each sweet sigh,
In chambers deep, our spirits fly.

Though miles may stretch, the bonds remain,
In every joy, in every pain.
A journey shared, though roads are wide,
Through valleys low, and mountains tried.

With quiet strength, we build and grow,
In tender light, the love will show.
Though parallel, we find our way,
In every dusk, in every day.

So trust the path that fate will weave,
In heart's embrace, we learn to believe.
For in the distance, love will chart,
The parallel journeys of the heart.

Swimming in the Depths of Thought

Beneath the waves, my mind will dive,
Where currents of ideas twist and thrive.
In murky depths, some fears arise,
Yet still I seek the sunlit skies.

Each bubble forms a fleeting dream,
A shimmer bright, a silver beam.
I navigate through storm and calm,
To find the peace, my heart's sweet balm.

The depths may swirl, the shadows loom,
Yet I embrace the hidden room.
With every stroke, I learn my way,
To merge the night with breaking day.

What treasures hide in ocean's heart?
What wisdom speaks in depths apart?
I chase the echoes, soft and clear,
Each thought a whisper, sweet and near.

As tides will shift, and thoughts may fade,
I'll linger still, unafraid,
For in this space, I come alive,
In swimming, I shall truly thrive.

Dances with the Ghosts of Memory

In shadows cast, the memories twirl,
Each moment lived, a fleeting pearl.
With every step, I feel their sway,
The ghosts of time, come out to play.

They waltz through halls of faded light,
In whispers soft, they hold me tight.
I swirl and spin in haunting grace,
Embracing all, each time and place.

They laugh and weep, both joy and pain,
In echoes sweet, they still remain.
A bittersweet, familiar song,
In dances where we all belong.

So let me dance, both slow and fast,
With every specter from the past.
Together we forge a timeless thread,
In shadows deep, where dreams are fed.

For in the dance, I find my truth,
The tapestry of love and youth.
These ghosts remind me who I am,
In every heartbeat, every slam.

Palette of Internal Landscapes

Colors blend in mind's vast space,
A canvas rich, where thoughts embrace.
With strokes of passion, hues of grace,
I paint the worlds that I can trace.

Mountains rise with shades of bold,
In valleys deep, soft stories told.
The rivers flow with dreams anew,
Each brush a glimpse of all I knew.

Fields of gold beneath the sun,
Whispering tales of all I've done.
A forest thick with quiet sighs,
Each tree a witness to my cries.

I wander through this vivid dream,
Where every shadow holds a gleam.
In every corner, life unfolds,
With vibrant visions, hopes, and golds.

So let me paint, let colors sing,
In this realm, my heart takes wing.
A palette rich, forever true,
In internal lands, I start anew.

Crossing the Bridges of Self

Each bridge I cross, a choice to make,
The paths diverge, but I won't break.
I stand and breathe, embrace the fear,
For every step, my heart stays clear.

With wooden planks and steel so strong,
Each bridge a verse of my life's song.
Through winding paths, I search my soul,
To find the pieces that make me whole.

I walk with courage, leave the doubt,
In every heartbeat, I shout out.
The spans may shake, but I will stand,
To claim the destiny I've planned.

With every step, new vistas form,
Amidst the quiet and the storm.
Each bridge reflects a truth inside,
A guiding light, my faithful guide.

So here's to crossing, bold and free,
In bridges built, I find the key.
With every leap, I come to know,
The journey's worth, the strength to grow.

Secrets in the Silence

In the hush of night, whispers gleam,
Shadows dance in a forgotten dream.
Breath held tight, hearts softly pound,
Quiet truths in the stillness found.

Beneath the stars where secrets lie,
Echoes of souls that dare to fly.
Silent songs of what's unseen,
Life's delicate thread woven between.

A gaze into the silent void,
Moments cherished, yet destroyed.
Fingers trace a memory's edge,
In silence, comfort is our pledge.

Unspoken words float above,
Wrapped in layers, cradled by love.
Time ticks slow; the world stands still,
In silence, we feel life's thrill.

The echoes fade, yet linger on,
A gentle kiss, a hidden dawn.
Secrets bloom where silence reigns,
In stillness, freedom breaks the chains.

The Heart's Hidden Atlas

Maps drawn in the folds of skin,
Paths unexplored where dreams begin.
The heart beats strong, a guide so true,
Tracing routes to depths anew.

Worn edges of love's ancient tome,
In every chapter, we find our home.
Journeys taken, stones left unturned,
Lessons learned, and passions burned.

Twists and turns through joy and strife,
The compass spins, revealing life.
In every scar, a story sings,
The heart whispers of fragile wings.

Through valleys low and peaks so high,
The atlas breathes, a constant sigh.
With every pulse, it charts our fate,
Guiding us through love's vast state.

Where shadows loom and sunlight gleams,
In the heart's map, we chase our dreams.
A hidden path, yet deeply known,
In every step, we're never alone.

Melodies of the Soul's Journey

Notes that linger in the air,
Strumming strings of deep despair.
Yet with each chord, hope rises high,
Infusing dreams that never die.

In the rhythm of each heartbeat,
We find the strength to stand on our feet.
Melodies play in twilight's glow,
Guiding us through pain and woe.

A choir of voices, dark and bright,
Echoing truths found in the light.
Harsh dissonance turns into grace,
In every tune, we find our place.

The dance of life, both swift and slow,
Carrying us where we need to go.
With every rise, a fall to claim,
Each note a whisper, a sacred name.

So let the music paint the sky,
With colors bold, we learn to fly.
In every melody, our souls run free,
A symphony born of you and me.

Reaching for the Stars Within

Fingers stretch toward midnight skies,
Yearning dreams in every sigh.
Stars twinkle with a distant light,
Awakening hope in the quiet night.

Hearts aspire to heights untold,
In the shadows, ambitions unfold.
Dreams ignite like celestial fire,
A radiant spark to lift us higher.

Echoing thoughts on cosmic winds,
Destinies plotted where starlight spins.
Each heartbeat a step on the way,
Guided by the dawn of a new day.

Among the galaxies we soar,
With every breath, we crave for more.
The cosmos whispers secrets sweet,
In every journey, we find our feet.

So reach deep within, find your star,
For light resides both near and far.
The universe dances in your soul,
In reaching, we discover the whole.

The Silent Journey to Self-Discovery

In quiet whispers, truths unfold,
Beneath the layers, heartbeats bold.
Step by step through shadows cast,
A journey inward, home at last.

Each thought a step, each breath a guide,
In the stillness, fears subside.
A mirror held to see the light,
Reflections spark in darkest night.

With every choice, the soul awakes,
Embracing all the paths it takes.
The compass points to what is real,
In silence, we begin to heal.

Lessons learned in gentle streams,
We walk the path of waking dreams.
The heart expands where love resides,
In the quiet, the truth abides.

The journey flows like rivers wide,
Through valleys deep, the spirit's ride.
In every heartbeat, we become,
The silent journey leads us home.

Driftwood Memories

Pieces of time, washed ashore,
Reminders of life, stories and more.
Weathered and worn by ocean's grace,
Each one holds a familiar face.

Carried by currents, lost and found,
Echoes of laughter, love profound.
In the grains of wood, tales entwine,
Crafted by waves, like aged wine.

The sea's soft sigh, a siren's song,
In driftwood dreams, we all belong.
Fragments of joy, sorrows released,
Nature's embrace, memory's feast.

With every tide, the past returns,
In shifting sands, the spirit yearns.
To hold the fleeting moments dear,
In driftwood's arms, we disappear.

Lost in the stories the waters tell,
Of distant shores where we once fell.
Fragments linger, hearts connect,
In driftwood memories, we reflect.

The Unfurling of Inner Horizons

In the dawn of thought, horizons stretch,
Breath by breath, the mind can etch.
Petals unfold, revealing bright
The colors hidden in morning light.

Awakening dreams, like whispers rise,
Chasing the depth of boundless skies.
Each thought a seed, each hope a sun,
Together they bloom; the journey's begun.

Across the vastness, possibilities gleam,
In the tapestry of every dream.
The inner world, a canvas grand,
Just waiting for the artist's hand.

Unfurling visions, delicate grace,
In shadows cast, we find our place.
Embracing chance, we leap and soar,
Horizons beckon, calling for more.

With hearts unbound, we face the dawn,
In the unfurling, we are reborn.
Together we travel, side by side,
In endless journeys, love the guide.

The Depths Where Secrets Dwell

In the ocean's heart, shadows play,
Where whispered thoughts drift away.
Beneath the waves, in silence bound,
Secrets sleep, where none are found.

Each tide reveals a hidden truth,
In cryptic depths, a quest for youth.
Treasures buried, waiting for light,
In the depths, where day meets night.

The echoes call from ages past,
Mysterious tales in silence cast.
With every ripple, memories sway,
In depths of stillness, lost at play.

The water's depth, a world unknown,
Where fears and hopes have freely grown.
In shadows cast, reflections blend,
In the depths, we make our mend.

As we dive into the silent swell,
We find the strength in secrets' spell.
Embracing darkness, we may find,
In depths where secrets dwell, we're aligned.

Currents of the Unconscious

Whispers drift beneath the waves,
Where shadows play in velvet caves.
Thoughts emerge, a silent tide,
Carried forth where secrets hide.

Dreams like fish in currents flow,
In depths of mind, they ebb and glow.
Echoes linger, soft and low,
In the depths where feelings grow.

Ripples dance on waters gray,
Memories fade, then rise to sway.
Lost in thoughts, I drift away,
In twilight realms, forever stay.

Time slips through like grains of sand,
Fleeting moments, a gentle hand.
Guiding me through night's embrace,
To find myself in timeless space.

As the currents shift and change,
I watch the skies grow vast and strange.
Navigating through the deep,
Where hidden truths lie still, asleep.

A Quest Beneath the Skin

In the layers, whispers dwell,
Stories told, they weave a spell.
Searching for the heart's own beat,
In the shadows, we discreet.

Veins like rivers, pulse with fire,
Every throb, a deep desire.
Beneath the skin, a world unfolds,
A canvas rich with dreams and gold.

With every touch, a truth revealed,
A hidden realm, gently sealed.
In the silence, echoes near,
A symphony we long to hear.

The surface hides the deepest tales,
Where longing lingers, hope prevails.
In the quest, we find our grace,
Embracing what we can't erase.

A journey starts with every breath,
In life's embrace or whispered death.
Within us all, a treasure waits,
Exposing love, unlocking fates.

Mysterious Waters of the Soul

In darkened depths, reflections gleam,
A liquid mirror, a quiet dream.
Submerged in thoughts, I float and drift,
Searching for the quiet gift.

The waters swirl, they pull me close,
With every rush, I feel the prose.
Ink and waves in endless dance,
Lost within a fleeting glance.

Secrets buried in the foam,
In silent pools, I find my home.
The currents shift, they guide my heart,
In this dance, I'm set apart.

Glimmers shine beneath the surface,
Every ripple holds a purpose.
Through the depths, I start to see,
The essence of the soul's decree.

With every breath, I dive once more,
To unveil what lies in store.
Mysterious waters, deep and wide,
Within their folds, my truths abide.

The Inner Horizon Awaits

Beyond the veil, where dreams ignite,
An inner horizon, pure and bright.
With open eyes, I seek the dawn,
A pathway where the soul is drawn.

In the stillness, whispers rise,
Guiding me beneath the skies.
Every step, a new refrain,
Unraveling the joy and pain.

Mountains hush, the valleys sigh,
In their embrace, the echoes lie.
A journey reaches for the light,
As shadows play with day and night.

Through the mist, the vision clears,
A tapestry of hopes and fears.
The inner horizon stands in grace,
Inviting me to find my place.

In the distance, dreams take flight,
Illuminating paths of night.
With every heartbeat, I await,
The dawn that promises my fate.

9 781805 609568